DIMENSIONS, WEIGHTS,

AND

TRACTIVE POWER

OF

NARROW-GAUGE LOCOMOTIVES,

MANUFACTURED BY THE

BALDWIN LOCOMOTIVE WORKS.

BURNHAM, PARRY, WILLIAMS & CO.,

PHILADELPHIA, PA.

PRESS OF
J. B. LIPPINCOTT & CO.
1877.

©2007-2010 Periscope Film LLC
All Rights Reserved
ISBN 978-1-935700-12-8
www.PeriscopeFilm.com

BALDWIN LOCOMOTIVE WORKS.

Burnham, Parry, Williams & Co.,

PHILADELPHIA, PA.,

Manufacturers of

LOCOMOTIVE ENGINES

OF EVERY DESCRIPTION, FOR BOTH

WIDE AND NARROW-GAUGE RAILWAYS.

GEORGE BURNHAM,	EDWARD H. WILLIAMS,	EDWARD LONGSTRETH,
CHARLES T. PARRY,	WILLIAM P. HENSZEY,	JOHN H. CONVERSE.

CIRCULAR.

We present herewith photographs and figures showing the patterns, dimensions, and tractive power of various classes of locomotives for narrow-gauge railways.

All the classes of locomotives specified can be built for the United States standard narrow gauge of three feet, the South American standard narrow gauge of one metre, the Canadian standard narrow gauge of three and one-half feet, or for any intermediate or wider gauge.

All work is accurately fitted to gauges and templets, which are made from a system of standards kept exclusively for the purpose. Like parts will, therefore, fit accurately in all locomotives of the same class.

This system of manufacture is a distinctive feature of these Works. Its value and importance to the *users of locomotives* cannot be overestimated. By its means the expense of maintenance and repairs is reduced to a minimum. A company whose railroad is equipped with our locomotives may save, almost wholly, all outlays for shops, machinery, drawings, and patterns for their repairs. The necessity of maintaining for the same purpose an organization of skilled workmen at a constant expense is also obviated. Every important part of the locomotive being accurately made to a templet, we can at any time supply a duplicate part, made to the same templet, which is sure to fit in the place of the original. The large number of locomotives at all times in progress, and embracing the principal classes, insures unusual and especial facilities for filling at once, or with the least possible delay, orders for such duplicate parts.

It will also be apparent that a company procuring its equipment of motive power at these Works, can, at the same time, supply itself with a limited stock of duplicate parts sufficient for all repairs likely to be required. An expenditure of a *few hundred dollars* in this manner will provide more fully and perfectly for all ordinary contingencies than would a large investment of capital in shops, machinery, and organization designed for the same purpose.

The important saving possible by this method will manifest itself in two directions:

1. The first cost of the necessary parts for repairs will be from 25 to 50 *per cent.* less than if made in the railroad company's shop. We are constantly producing such parts by workmen trained by long experience in each specialty, and hence with the greatest economy in expenditure both of labor and material.

2. The services of the engine are lost for the shortest possible time while undergoing repairs. Having already on hand the necessary part, the master mechanic can at once apply it.

Otherwise a force of workmen must be maintained at a constant and large expense in order to be in readiness to manufacture the required parts when the occasion arises; and when the demand comes, the use of the engine must be lost for a considerable time while perhaps drawings or patterns are made, and from them the proper parts constructed and fitted in place.

The *loads* given under each class are invariably in gross tons of 2240 pounds, and include both cars and lading. All the locomotives described are sold with the guarantee that they will haul the loads stated on a straight track in good condition, assuming the resistance of the cars not to exceed ten pounds per ton of 2240 pounds of their weight.

Designs and estimates for any other required patterns of locomotives will be submitted on application.

The delivery of locomotives at any point which can be reached by rail or vessel will be included in contracts if desired.

For detailed specifications and further particulars, address

Burnham, Parry, Williams & Co.,

PHILADELPHIA, PA.

Explanation of Class Designations.

Each class of locomotives is designated by two figures, or sets of figures, separated by a hyphen, and combined with the letter C, D, or E.

The figure before the hyphen indicates the whole number of wheels under the locomotive; the figure after the hyphen, the diameter of cylinders, thus:

The figures 10½ are used to designate cylinders 8 inches in diam.
" 11 & 12 " " " 9 " "
" 14 " " " 10 " "
" 16 " " " 11 " "
" 18 " " " 12 " "
" 20 " " " 13 " "
" 22 " " " 14 " "
" 24 " " " 15 " "

[The fraction ¼ added to any of these figures indicates that the locomotive has a truck at each end, making it a "Double-Ender." The fraction ½ indicates a special class.]

The letter C indicates that 4 wheels are connected as driving wheels.

The letter D indicates that 6 wheels are connected as driving-wheels.

The letter E indicates that 8 wheels are connected as driving-wheels.

Thus, 8-14 C means an 8-wheeled locomotive having cylinders 10 inches in diameter and 4 driving-wheels; 8-16 D, an 8-wheeled locomotive having cylinders 11 inches in diameter and 6 driving-wheels; and 10-22 E, a 10-wheeled locomotive having cylinders 14 inches in diameter and 8 driving-wheels.

NARROW-GAUGE PASSENGER LOCOMOTIVE.

CLASS 8-14 C.

General design illustrated by photograph of the "No. 2," on page 9.

CYLINDERS . . 10 inches diameter, 16 inches stroke.
DRIVING-WHEELS . . . 38 to 42 inches diameter.
TRUCK-WHEELS . 24 inches diameter, with centre-bearing swinging or sliding bolster.
WHEEL-BASE, total . . . . 18 feet.
" rigid . (distance between driving-wheel centres) . . . 6 feet 9 inches.
TENDER, four-wheeled . . tank capacity, 700 gallons.
" eight-wheeled . . " " 1000 "

WEIGHT OF ENGINE IN WORKING ORDER.

On drivers . . . . . . 22,000 pounds.
On truck . . . . . . 11,000 "

Total weight of engine . . . 33,000 "

LOAD.

IN GROSS TONS OF CARS AND LADING.

On a level . . . . . . 525 gross tons.
" 20 feet grade . . . . . 245 " "
" 40 " " . . . . . 150 " "
" 60 " " . . . . . 105 " "
" 80 " " . . . . . 80 " "
" 100 " " . . . . . 65 " "

Narrow-Gauge Passenger Locomotive.

CLASS 8-16 C.

General design illustrated by photograph of "No. 2," on page 9.

CYLINDERS . . 11 inches diameter, 16 inches stroke.
DRIVING-WHEELS . . . 38 to 42 inches diameter.
TRUCK-WHEELS . 24 inches diameter, with centre-bearing swinging or sliding bolster.
WHEEL-BASE, total . . . . . 18 feet 5 inches.
" rigid . (distance between driving-wheel centres) . . . 7 feet 2 inches.
TENDER, four-wheeled . . tank capacity, 750 gallons.
" eight-wheeled . . " " 1100 "

WEIGHT OF ENGINE IN WORKING ORDER.

On drivers . . . . . 24,000 pounds.
On truck . . . . . 12,000 "

Total weight of engine . . . 36,000 "

LOAD

IN GROSS TONS OF CARS AND LADING.

On a level . . . . . . 600 gross tons.
" 20 feet grade . . . . . 280 " "
" 40 " " . . . . . 175 " "
" 60 " " . . . . . 125 " "
" 80 " " . . . . . 95 " "
" 100 " " . . . . . 75 " "

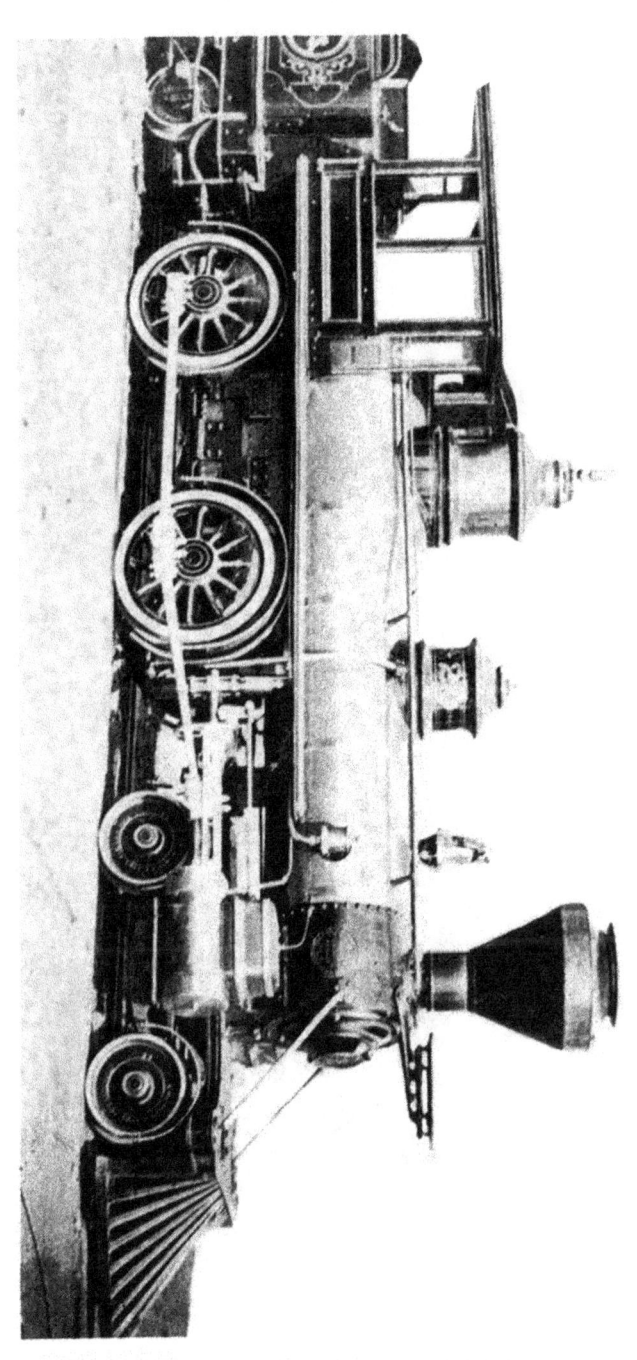

10

NARROW-GAUGE PASSENGER LOCOMOTIVE.

CLASS 8-18 C.

General design illustrated by photograph of the "Schuylkill," on page 10.

CYLINDERS	12 inches diameter, 16 inch stroke.
DRIVING-WHEELS	38 to 42 inches diameter.
TRUCK-WHEELS	24 inches diameter, with centre-bearing swinging or sliding bolster.
WHEEL-BASE, total	18 feet 9 inches.
" rigid	(distance between driving-wheel centres) . . . 7 feet 6 inches.
TENDER, four-wheeled	tank capacity, 800 gallons.
" eight-wheeled	" " 1200 "

WEIGHT OF ENGINE IN WORKING ORDER.

On drivers	27,000 pounds.
On truck	13,000 "
Total weight of engine	40,000 "

LOAD.

IN GROSS TONS OF CARS AND LADING.

On a level	670 gross tons.
" 20 feet grade	310 " "
" 40 " "	195 " "
" 60 " "	140 " "
" 80 " "	105 " "
" 100 " "	85 " "

NARROW-GAUGE PASSENGER LOCOMOTIVE.

CLASS 8-20 C.

General design illustrated by photograph of the "Schuylkill," on page 10.

CYLINDERS . . 13 inches diameter, 16 or 18 inches stroke.
DRIVING-WHEELS . . . . 42 to 48 inches diameter.
TRUCK-WHEELS . 24 to 26 inches diameter, with centre-bearing swinging or sliding bolster.
WHEEL-BASE, total . . . . . 19 feet 1 inch.
" rigid (distance between driving-wheel centres) . . . 7 feet 10 inches.
TENDER, eight-wheeled . . tank capacity, 1400 gallons.

WEIGHT OF ENGINE IN WORKING ORDER.

On drivers . . . . . . 31,000 pounds.
On truck . . . . . . 14,000 "

Total weight of engine . . . 45,000 "

LOAD.

IN GROSS TONS OF CARS AND LADING.

On a level . . . . . 740 gross tons.
" 20 feet grade . . . . 340 " "
" 40 " " . . . . . 215 " "
" 60 " " . . . . . 155 " "
" 80 " " . . . . . 115 " "
" 100 " " . . . . . 90 " "

REMARKS.

The four preceding classes of locomotives are designed especially for passenger service, and can be run at speeds of from 25 to 40 miles per hour.

Classes 8–14 C and 8–16 C are adapted for service on light rails weighing from 30 to 35 pounds per yard. For service on tracks laid with heavier rails, Classes 8–18 C and 8–20 C are recommended. It may be noted, however, that the locomotive "Schuylkill" (photograph on page 10), Class 8–18 C, was run on 35 pound rails on the narrow-gauge passenger railway in the Centennial Exhibition grounds, from May to November, 1876.

On the Nevada County (3 feet gauge) Railroad, of California, on which the maximum grade is 116 feet per mile, a locomotive of Class 8–16 C hauls six loaded eight-wheeled cars. Weight of each loaded car, 9 gross tons. Total weight of train, 54 gross tons.

On the Camden, Gloucester and Mount Ephraim Railway, 3 feet gauge (laid with 30 and 35 pound rails), a locomotive of the same class has hauled five loaded eight-wheeled freight cars and two loaded passenger cars up a grade of 110 feet per mile.

The usual train is two passenger cars, with which the run is made from Gloucester to Camden, two miles, in eight minutes, making one intermediate stop, and running slow into the city of Camden. One curve of only 120 feet radius occurs on entering Camden.

On the Denver and Rio Grande Railway, passenger locomotives of Class 8–16 C take the regular passenger trains of three cars at a speed of 20 miles per hour on all grades, the maximum being 75 feet per mile. For full particulars of their performance on this line, see letter of W. W. Borst, Superintendent, on pages 25 and 26.

On the Eureka and Palisade Railroad (3 feet gauge), of Nevada, a locomotive of Class 8–18 C, with one passenger coach attached, has made the run from Palisade to Eureka, 90 miles, in two hours and thirty-eight minutes, nearly all the distance being up grade, viz.: 52 feet per mile for 35 miles, 75 feet per mile for 8 miles, and 105 feet per mile for 3 miles. Average speed, 34.17 miles per hour.

We subjoin copy of a statement by the General Manager of the Centennial Narrow-Gauge Railway, showing the performance of a passenger locomotive of Class 8–18 C, and of a freight locomotive of Class 8–18 D, on the Narrow-Gauge Railway in the Centennial Exhibition grounds from May to November, 1876:

WEST END PASSENGER RAILWAY CO.,
PHILADELPHIA, November 30, 1876.

Messrs. BURNHAM, PARRY, WILLIAMS & CO.,
Baldwin Locomotive Works, Philadelphia.

GENTLEMEN:

During the Centennial Exhibition we have had in use on our three-feet gauge railroad in the Exhibition grounds two of your locomotives, one being Class 8-18 C, and one Class 8-18 D, both of which have given entire satisfaction under such circumstances as locomotives are seldom made to perform.

These engines came under my daily supervision and did their full share in transporting over *four millions* of passengers on this now famous little railway.

The gauge of the line was three feet, with double track three and a half miles long, or seven miles in all. For its length it was probably the most crooked road in the world, being made up almost wholly of curves, in order to run near all the principal buildings on the Exhibition grounds. Many of these curves were on our heaviest grades, some having a radius of 215, 230, and 250 feet on grades of 140 and 155 feet per mile. These are unusually heavy grades and curves, and when *combined* as we had them, with only a 35 pound iron rail, made the task for our engines exceedingly difficult.

Your locomotive "Schuylkill," Class 8-18 C, began service May 13, and made 156 days to the close of Exhibition. The locomotive "Delaware," Class 8-18 D, came into service

June 9, and made 131 days to the close of the Exhibition. The usual load of each engine was five eight-wheeled passenger cars, frequently carrying over 100 passengers per car. On special occasions as many as six and seven loaded cars have been drawn by one of these engines.

Each engine averaged fully sixteen trips daily, equal to fifty-six miles, and, as the stations were but a short distance apart, the Westinghouse air-brake was applied in making 160 daily stops, or a total of 25,000 for each engine. Neither engine was out of service an hour unless from accidents for which they were in no way responsible.

Very respectfully,

(Signed)   R. W. FLOWER, Jr.,
General Manager.

[NOTE.—Average weight of each loaded car, about 12 gross tons.]

NARROW-GAUGE FREIGHT LOCOMOTIVE.

CLASS 8-16 D.

General design illustrated by photographs of the "Delaware" and "M. Werk," on pages 19 and 20.

CYLINDERS	11 inches diameter, 16 inches stroke.
DRIVING-WHEELS	36 to 40 inches diameter.
TRUCK-WHEELS	24 inches diameter, with swinging or sliding bolster and radius-bar.
WHEEL-BASE, total	17 feet 4 inches.
" rigid	(distance between centres of front and back driving-wheels) 11 feet 4 inches.
TENDER, eight-wheeled	tank capacity, 1000 gallons.

WEIGHT OF ENGINE IN WORKING ORDER.

On drivers	29,000 pounds.
On truck	6,000 "
Total weight of engine	35,000 "

LOAD.

IN GROSS TONS OF CARS AND LADING.

On a level	720 gross tons.
" 20 feet grade	335 " "
" 40 " "	210 " "
" 60 " "	150 " "
" 80 " "	110 " "
" 100 " "	90 " "

Narrow-Gauge Freight Locomotive.

CLASS 8-18 D.

Illustrated by photographs of the "Delaware" and "M. Werk," on pages 19 and 20.

CYLINDERS . 12 inches diameter, 16 or 18 inches stroke.
DRIVING-WHEELS . . . 36 to 40 inches diameter.
TRUCK-WHEELS . 24 inches diameter, with swinging or sliding bolster and radius-bar.
WHEEL-BASE, total . . . . . 17 feet 8 inches.
    " rigid . (distance between centres of front and back driving-wheels) 11 feet 8 inches.
TENDER, eight-wheeled . . tank capacity, 1200 gallons.

WEIGHT OF ENGINE IN WORKING ORDER.

On drivers . . . . . . 33,000 pounds.
On truck . . . . . . 6,000 "

    Total weight of engine . . . 39,000 "

LOAD.

IN GROSS TONS OF CARS AND LADING.

On a level . . . . . . 840 gross tons.
  " 20 feet grade . . . . 390 " "
  " 40 " " . . . . . 250 " "
  " 60 " " . . . . . 180 " "
  " 80 " " . . . . . 135 " "
  " 100 " " . . . . . 110 " "

20

NARROW-GAUGE FREIGHT LOCOMOTIVE.

CLASS 8-20 D.

Illustrated by photographs of the "Delaware" and "M. Werk," on pages 19 and 20.

CYLINDERS . 13 inches diameter, 16 or 18 inches stroke.
DRIVING-WHEELS . . . 36 to 40 inches diameter.
TRUCK-WHEELS . 24 inches diameter, with swinging or sliding bolster and radius-bar.
WHEEL-BASE, total . . . . . . 18 feet.
" rigid . (distance between centres of front and back driving-wheels) 12 feet.
TENDER, eight-wheeled . . tank capacity, 1400 gallons.

WEIGHT OF ENGINE IN WORKING ORDER.

On drivers . . . . . . 37,000 pounds.
On truck . . . . . . 7,000 "
                                             ———
Total weight of engine . . . 44,000 "

LOAD.

IN GROSS TONS OF CARS AND LADING.

On a level . . . . . . 965 gross tons.
" 20 feet grade . . . . . 445 " "
" 40   "   "   . . . . . 285 " "
" 60   "   "   . . . . . 205 " "
" 80   "   "   . . . . . 160 " "
" 100 "   "   . . . . . 125 " "

Narrow-Gauge Freight Locomotive.

CLASS 8-22 D.

Illustrated by photographs of the "Delaware" and "M. Werk," on pages 19 and 20.

Cylinders . . 14 inches diameter, 16 inches stroke, or 13 inches diameter, 18 inches stroke.
Driving-Wheels . . . 36 to 40 inches diameter.
Truck-Wheels . 24 inches diameter, with swinging or sliding bolster and radius-bar.
Wheel-Base, total . . . . . 18 feet 5 inches.
" rigid . (distance between centres of front and back driving-wheels) 12 feet 5 inches.
Tender, eight-wheeled . tank capacity, 1400 to 1600 gallons.

WEIGHT OF ENGINE IN WORKING ORDER.

On drivers	41,000 pounds.
On truck	7,000 "
Total weight of engine . . .	48,000 "

LOAD.

IN GROSS TONS OF CARS AND LADING.

On a level	1000 gross tons.
" 20 feet grade	470 " "
" 40 " "	300 " "
" 60 " "	215 " "
" 80 " "	165 " "
" 100 " "	130 " "

REMARKS.

The four preceding classes are designed especially for freight service, and can be adapted to the use of either wood or coal as fuel.

Classes 8–16 D and 8–18 D, having a weight on each driving-axle of from 10,000 to 11,000 pounds, are recommended for service on light rails weighing from 30 to 35 pounds per yard. Classes 8–20 D and 8–22 D, with a weight of from 12,000 to 14,000 pounds on each driving-axle, would require heavier rails.

The construction of these engines is such that they will readily pass short curves, the pony-truck having a swing-bolster and radius-bar, and the middle pair of driving-wheels having tires without flanges.

The Bell's Gap Railroad (of Pennsylvania), which is laid with 35 pound rails, and has a maximum grade of 158.4 feet per mile, combined with curves of 204 feet radius, is worked by two locomotives of Class 8–16 D. Thirty-three to thirty-five empty coal cars (weight of each car 2150 to 2200 pounds) can be taken by one engine up the grade and around the curves named.

On the Centennial Narrow-Gauge Railway a locomotive of Class 8–18 D, with a rigid wheel-base of 11 feet 8 inches, worked with entire success on curves of 215, 230, and 250 feet radius, combined with grades of 140 and 155 feet per mile. Over this track the regular load (as will be seen from the official statement printed on page 15) was five eight-wheeled passenger cars, each car frequently containing 100 passengers. No test was ever made, however, to show the maximum capacity of the engine in tractive power.

The Lake Tahoe (3 feet gauge) Railway, which has curves of 318 feet radius, is worked with three locomotives of Class 8–20 D. The rigid wheel-base of two of the engines is 12 feet 9 inches, and of the third, 12 feet.

We subjoin a letter giving particulars of the performance of freight locomotives (Class 8–18 D) and passenger locomotives (Class 8–16 C) on the Denver and Rio Grande Railway. The maximum grades on this line between Denver and Colorado Springs are 75 feet per mile, and the track is laid with 30 pound iron rails.

DENVER AND RIO GRANDE RAILWAY.

Office of Superintendent,

DENVER, COLORADO, February 13, 1877.

GENERAL WM. J. PALMER,

President D. and R. G. Railway Co.

DEAR SIR:

In reply to letter of Burnham, Parry, Williams & Co., in reference to the performance of our last engines, I have to say:

1. Freight engines Nos. 13, 14, 15, and 19 [Class 8-18 D]. The average train for these engines is twelve loaded box or thirteen loaded coal cars and caboose; each load 8 tons (coal cars 3½ tons, box cars 4 tons), or 150 tons of cars and lading, at a speed of 8 to 10 miles per hour.

Our average freight train time on present card is 10 miles per hour between Denver and Pueblo. On heavy grades the speed is reduced to 8 miles, and on slightly descending grades and levels the speed is increased to 12 miles.

We have, when rail and cars were in perfect condition, hauled fifteen loaded cars at about 6 miles per hour.

2. Passenger engines Nos. 16, 17, 18 [Class 8-16 C]. These engines are used on our regular passenger trains, consisting of one baggage car and two coaches, at a speed of 20 miles per hour on all grades. We have never had occasion to test either the speed or the power of these engines in passenger train service.

On the 29th of August, 1876, engine 16 took one baggage

car, five coaches, and one excursion car from Denver to Colorado Springs. Time, including stops, 4 hours; actual running time about 3½ hours. She did her work with ease, making 20 miles per hour on the heaviest grades. I am satisfied that either of the four-wheeled-connected passenger engines will haul seven coaches and one baggage car over our 75 feet grades at from 18 to 20 miles per hour.

These engines are as heavy as should be run over a 30 pound iron rail, although I do not see that they injure the iron more than our lighter engines.

When the road bed is soft these engines knock the track out of line more than our first engines.

Respectfully yours,

(Signed)   W. W. BORST,
Superintendent.

The following letter from Charles E. Holland, Esq , President of the Mineral Range Railroad Co., of Michigan, is especially interesting as furnishing valuable data respecting the performance of 3 feet gauge "Mogul" locomotives on exceptionally heavy grades, and in contending with deep and long-continued snows.

The three locomotives referred to, and with which this line is worked, are of the following classes:

The PORTAGE LAKE, Class 8–16 D, page 17 ; cylinders, 11 × 16 ; drivers, 36 inches diameter ; weight, 35,000 pounds.

The J. C. Sharpless, Class 8–18 D, page 18; cylinders, 12×16; drivers, 36 inches diameter; weight, 38,250 pounds.

The Keweenaw, Class 8–18 D, page 18; cylinders, 12 × 16; drivers, 40 inches diameter; weight, 40,000 pounds.

The Keweenaw and Sharpless are both of same class, but the former has a boiler 2 inches larger in diameter, and driving-wheels 4 inches larger in diameter.

MINERAL RANGE RAILROAD CO.,
Hancock, Mich., February 19, 1877.

Messrs. Burnham, Parry, Williams & Co.,
Philadelphia.

Gentlemen:

In reply to your inquiry relative to the working of the last engine furnished us, we would say that we use the "Sharpless" for freight service, the "Portage Lake" for passenger service, and the "Keweenaw" as a spare engine. I will give you the service of the "Sharpless," from which we can judge of the "Keweenaw" by comparison.

Our road is 12½ miles long. We leave the station at Hancock on a grade of 211 feet to the mile, which continues for a distance of about 1200 feet. We pass from this 211 feet grade to one of 146 feet to the mile, which latter grade continues for a distance of about 2 miles; after which the maximum grade is 60 feet to the mile, reaching an altitude at Calumet, the other end of the road, of 630 feet above the starting point. The curve of 410 feet radius occurs upon the 146 feet grade.

The snow commences falling in November usually, and continues to fall steadily until January or February, with occasional heavy storms after that time, with high winds and heavy drifts. Sleighing comes with the first fall of snow, and continues until April, and sometimes until the early part of May. By 1st January we have from 1½ to 3 feet of snow, and it is not an unusual thing to find 3½ to 4 feet of snow in the woods on the 1st of April. This is our average winter. The present winter is the mildest we have experienced since 1857 and '8.

During the winter of 1875, with very heavy snows, high winds, and the mercury ranging from 0 to 35 below for over 40 days, we were only delayed, all told, about 3 days; that is, the Smelting Works and Stamp (Crushing) Mills, to which we brought their daily supplies of material, were stopped, on account of our inability to get trains through, only about 3 days.

In exposed places on the 146 feet grade the snow often drifts to the depth of 3½ to 5 feet on the track, and becomes so hard that one could walk upon it as easily as upon a floor. With the "Sharpless" provided with a small iron plow, we have often worked up grade, clearing the road of these drifts, and to good effect. She would go into them for a distance of 200 to 500 feet each run, before the snow would stop her by getting under the drivers and causing the engine to slip.

With this explanation of the difficulties we are called upon to surmount in operating our road, you will be able to judge intelligently of the service of the engines. We are now hauling about 90,000 tons of freight per annum, or at that rate, say 12,000 tons from Hancock up grade, and 70,000 tons of copper rock, and 8000 tons of copper down grade. The copper is transported upon 8-wheeled freight cars, and the rock in 8-wheeled hopper cars, the cars weighing each $6\frac{1}{4}$ tons empty, and $18\frac{3}{4}$ tons loaded.

The "Sharpless" [12 × 16 cylinders, 36 in. drivers] will draw up the 211 feet grade 10 empty hopper cars. Total weight, $62\frac{1}{2}$ tons. On the 146 feet grade, which includes the curve of 410 feet radius, with a good rail, the same engine draws regularly 12 empty hopper cars. Total weight, 75 tons.

Its usual load on the 60 feet grade is 12 empty rock cars and 6 loaded freight cars. Weight, about 150 tons "going up." The usual down freight train consists of 12 loaded rock cars, and from 6 to 8 cars of copper. Weight of cars and lading, say for 18 cars, 305 tons; 20 cars, 332 tons.

This is our regular work, unless the rail is unusually bad by reason of snow or frost.

The capacity of the "Keweenaw" [12 × 16 cylinders, 40 in. drivers], on the 211 and 146 feet grades, is about 6 to 12 tons less, as near as we can judge. For freight service we consider the "Sharpless" the best; for passenger service the "Keweenaw" excels; the larger boiler causes her to steam easily, and her greater weight to run very steadily.

The "Portage Lake" [11 × 16 cylinders, 36 in. drivers] draws 2 coaches, weight 15 tons, and 1 freight car, weight, say 12 to 14 tons, and makes the trip from Hancock to Calumet in

50 minutes. Deducting stops, this would make running time about 40 to 45 minutes. We use this engine in passenger service, as the other engines, being larger, are more desirable for heavy work.

We consider that with the "Sharpless" we can transport in one year, making 2 round trips over the road per day, 100,000 tons of freight down grade, and 30,000 tons up grade, the work all to be done between 7 A.M. and 6 P.M., and by the "Sharpless" alone. By adding one more trip, time required 4 hours, the service would be increased 33 to 50 per cent.

Our rail weighs 35 pounds per yard, which we consider heavy enough for the engines. When we renew we shall use a heavier rail, and increase the weight of freight engines purchased in future.

To sum up, your engines have given perfect satisfaction, and we do not see in what manner they could be improved. Our service, with the grades, snow, and ice, is very hard, but the engines have never failed. I have written at length that you might fully understand what we were doing, and will be very glad to answer any further inquiries you may be pleased to make.

     Very truly yours,

(Signed)   CHARLES E. HOLLAND.

Narrow-Gauge Freight Locomotive.

CLASS 10-22 E.

Illustrated by photograph of the "No. 3," on page 33.

Cylinders . . 14 inches diameter, 16 inches stroke.
Driving-Wheels . . . . 36 inches diameter.
Truck-Wheels . 24 inches diameter, with sliding or swinging bolster and radius-bar.
Wheel-Base, total . . . . . 18 feet 2 inches.
" rigid . (distance between centres of first and fourth pairs of driving-wheels) 12 feet.
Tender, eight-wheeled . tank capacity, 1200 to 1400 gallons.

WEIGHT OF ENGINE IN WORKING ORDER.

On drivers . . . . . . 44,000 pounds.
On truck . . . . . . 8,000 "

Total weight of engine . . . 52,000 "

LOAD.

IN GROSS TONS OF CARS AND LADING.

On a level . . . . . . 1060 gross tons.
" 20 feet grade . . . . . 490 " "
" 40 " " . . . . . 310 " "
" 60 " " . . . . . 220 " "
" 80 " " . . . . . 175 " "
" 100 " " . . . . . 140 " "

Narrow-Gauge Freight Locomotive.

CLASS 10-24 E.

Illustrated by photograph of the "No. 3," on page 33.

CYLINDERS . . 15 inches diameter, 18 inches stroke.
DRIVING-WHEELS . . . . 36 inches diameter.
TRUCK-WHEELS . 24 inches diameter, with sliding or swinging bolster and radius-bar.
WHEEL-BASE, total . . . . . 18 feet 2 inches.
    " rigid . (distance between centres of first and fourth pairs of driving-wheels) 12 feet.
TENDER, eight-wheeled . tank capacity, 1400 to 1600 gallons.

WEIGHT OF ENGINE IN WORKING ORDER.

On drivers . . . . . . 50,000 pounds.
On truck . . . . . . 8,000 "
    Total weight of engine . . . 58,000 "

LOAD.

IN GROSS TONS OF CARS AND LADING.

On a level . . . . . . 1200 gross tons.
  " 20 feet grade . . . . . 560 " "
  " 40 " " . . . . . 355 " "
  " 60 " " . . . . . 255 " "
  " 80 " " . . . . . 195 " "
  " 100 " " . . . . . 155 " "

34

REMARKS.

The preceding classes of engines, known as the "Consolidation" pattern, are especially adapted to heavy freight service and to working steep gradients, as by utilizing the adhesion of four pairs of driving-wheels very great tractive power is obtained.

The pony-truck has a swinging or sliding bolster, allowing it to move laterally under the engine, and only two of the four pairs of drivers are flanged wheels. The engines will therefore readily pass short curves.

In Class 10–22 E, the distribution of the weight on four pairs of drivers places only about 11,000 pounds on each driving-axle. An engine of this class may therefore be used on rails weighing from 30 to 35 pounds per yard. For Class 10–24 E, the weight on each driving-wheel being about 12,500 pounds, it is believed rails weighing 40 pounds per yard will be found sufficient.

We subjoin by permission the following letters, showing the performance of locomotives of the "Consolidation" pattern on narrow-gauge railways:

OFFICE E. B. T. R. R. AND COAL CO.

ORBISONIA, August 6, 1875.

BURNHAM, PARRY, WILLIAMS & CO.

GENTLEMEN:

Your favor of the 4th inst. is received with regard to the performance of our Engines 3, 4, and 5 (Class 10–22 E, page 31).

Our maximum grade is 140 feet per mile, 3 miles in length. On this grade we have several curves 574' and 478' radius, one of 338', and several reverse curves of longer radius. The regular load of these engines, at a speed of 12 miles per hour, is 15 coal dumps weighing 9500 pounds each, with passenger car of 18,000 pounds, making total load, exclusive of tender, of $81\frac{1}{4}$ tons of 2000 pounds. The passenger car and 18 cars, loaded 10 tons each, or $274\frac{1}{2}$ tons, we consider a load on adverse grades of $52\frac{8}{10}$ feet per mile.

The above are not isolated cases, but is work actually done by the engines day after day, whenever the business of the road requires it.

As regards speed, I have run them on passenger trains at schedule time of 20 miles per hour with perfect ease and safety.

We have a curve of 240' radius on one of our branches, which these engines pass over easily.

Yours truly,

(Signed)   A. W. SIMS,

Superintendent.

[The following refers to locomotives of about the same weight as Class 10-24 E, page 32, but with cylinders 16 × 20, and driving-wheels 41 inches diameter.]

OFFICE TORONTO, GREY & BRUCE RAILWAY.

TORONTO, August 11, 1875.

Messrs. BURNHAM, PARRY, WILLIAMS & CO.

DEAR SIRS:

In answer to your favor of the 4th inst., I trust the following information may be of service to you.

The maximum loads of the class of engines you mention, Nos. 15 to 20, are 18 cars, giving a total load in gross tons of 270.

Our steepest grades are 88 feet per mile, having curves in combination of 10° and 13°.

Yours faithfully,

(Signed)   EDMUND WRAGGE.

NARROW-GAUGE FOUR-WHEELS-CONNECTED LOCOMOTIVES.

FOR SWITCHING OR FREIGHT SERVICE.

General design illustrated by photograph of the "Choctaw," on page 39.

Dimensions, weights, and tractive power of six different sizes of Locomotives to this pattern are given in the following table:

Class.	Cylinders, Diam. Stroke. Inches.	Drivers, Diam. Inches.	Weight in working order. Pounds.	LOAD IN GROSS TONS OF CARS AND LADING.					
				On a level.	20 feet grade.	40 feet grade.	60 feet grade.	80 feet grade.	100 feet grade.
4–10½ C	8 × 12	30	14,000	335	150	95	70	50	40
4–11 C	9 × 12	30	17,000	410	185	120	90	65	50
4–12 C	9 × 16	36	20,000	480	220	140	105	75	60
4–14 C	10 × 16	36	23,000	550	255	165	120	90	70
4–16 C	11 × 16	36	28,000	680	315	205	145	110	90
4–18 C	12 × 16	36	33,000	800	365	235	175	130	105

40

NARROW-GAUGE SIX-WHEELS-CONNECTED LOCOMOTIVES.

FOR SWITCHING OR FREIGHT SERVICE.

General design illustrated by photograph of the "B. G. R. R. No. 1," on page 40.

Dimensions, weights, and tractive power of seven different sizes of Locomotives to this pattern are given in the following table:

Class.	Cylinders, Diam. Stroke. Inches.	Drivers, Diam. Inches.	Weight in working order. Pounds.	LOAD IN GROSS TONS OF CARS AND LADING.				
				On a level.	20 feet grade.	40 feet grade.	60 feet grade.	80 feet grade.	100 feet grade.
6–11 D	9 × 12	30	19,000	410	185	120	90	65	50
6–12 D	9 × 16	36	22,000	480	220	140	105	75	60
6–14 D	10 × 16	36	25,000	550	255	165	120	90	70
6–16 D	11 × 16	36	31,000	680	315	205	145	110	90
6–18 D	12 × 16	36	36,000	800	365	235	175	130	105
6–20 D	13 × 16	36	40,000	900	430	275	200	150	120
6–22 D	14 × 16	36	44,000	1000	480	305	220	170	135

Narrow-Gauge Four-Wheels-Connected Tank Locomotives.

For Switching or Freight Service.

General design illustrated by photograph of the "España," on page 43.

Dimensions, weights, and tractive power of six different sizes of Engines to this pattern are given in the following table:

Class.	Cylinders, Diam. Stroke. Inches.	Drivers, Diam. Inches.	Weight in working order. Pounds.	LOAD IN GROSS TONS OF CARS AND LADING.					
				On a level.	20 feet grade.	40 feet grade.	60 feet grade.	80 feet grade.	100 feet grade.
4–10½ C	8 × 12	30	16,000	340	155	100	75	55	45
4–11 C	9 × 12	30	19,000	415	190	125	95	70	55
4–12 C	9 × 16	36	23,000	485	225	145	105	80	65
4–14 C	10 × 16	36	26,000	555	260	170	120	95	80
4–16 C	11 × 16	36	32,000	685	320	210	150	115	100
4–18 C	12 × 16	36	37,000	810	375	245	185	140	115

The weights given in the above table include water in tanks.

44

NARROW-GAUGE SIX-WHEELS-CONNECTED TANK LOCOMOTIVES,

FOR SWITCHING OR FREIGHT SERVICE.

General design illustrated by photograph of the "Millwood," on page 44.

Dimensions, weights, and tractive power of seven different sizes of Locomotives to this pattern are given in the following table:

Class.	Cylinders, Diam. Stroke. Inches.	Drivers, Diam. Inches.	Weight in working order. Pounds.	LOAD IN GROSS TONS OF CARS AND LADING.				
				On a level.	20 feet grade.	40 feet grade.	60 feet grade.	80 feet grade.	100 feet grade.
6-11 D	9 × 12	30	21,000	415	190	125	95	70	55
6-12 D	9 × 16	36	25,000	485	225	145	110	80	65
6-14 D	10 × 16	36	28,000	555	260	170	120	95	80
6-16 D	11 × 16	36	35,000	685	320	210	150	115	100
6-18 D	12 × 16	36	40,000	810	375	245	185	140	115
6-20 D	13 × 16	36	44,000	910	440	285	210	160	130
6-22 D	14 × 16	36	48,000	1000	490	315	230	180	145

The weights given in the above table include water in tanks.

Narrow-Gauge "Double-Ender" Tank Locomotives.

Designed to run either way without turning, and adapted to passenger service on short runs.

Plan illustrated by photograph of the "S. Sebastiao," on page 47.

Dimensions, weights, and tractive power of five different sizes of Locomotives to this pattern are given in the following table:

Class.	Cylinders, Diam. Stroke. Inches.	Drivers, Diam. Inches.	Weight in working order.		LOAD IN GROSS TONS OF CARS AND LADING.					
			Total.	On Drivers.	On a level.	20 feet grade.	40 feet grade.	60 feet grade.	80 feet grade.	100 feet grade.
8–10¼ C	8 × 12	36 to 40	22,000	12,000	270	125	85	60	45	35
8–12¼ C	9 × 16	36 to 40	30,000	18,000	420	200	125	90	65	50
8–14¼ C	10 × 16	36 to 40	36,000	23,000	540	260	165	120	85	65
8–16¼ C	11 × 16	36 to 40	42,000	28,000	650	315	205	145	110	90
8–18¼ C	12 × 16	36 to 40	47,000	31,000	720	350	230	160	125	100

Weights given above include weight of water in tank.

The leading and trailing wheels are arranged with swing-bolsters, so as to move laterally under the engine in passing curves. Engines of this class can therefore pass short curves without difficulty. One of class 8-10¼C is now working on a three-feet-gauge road with some curves of only 100 feet radius.

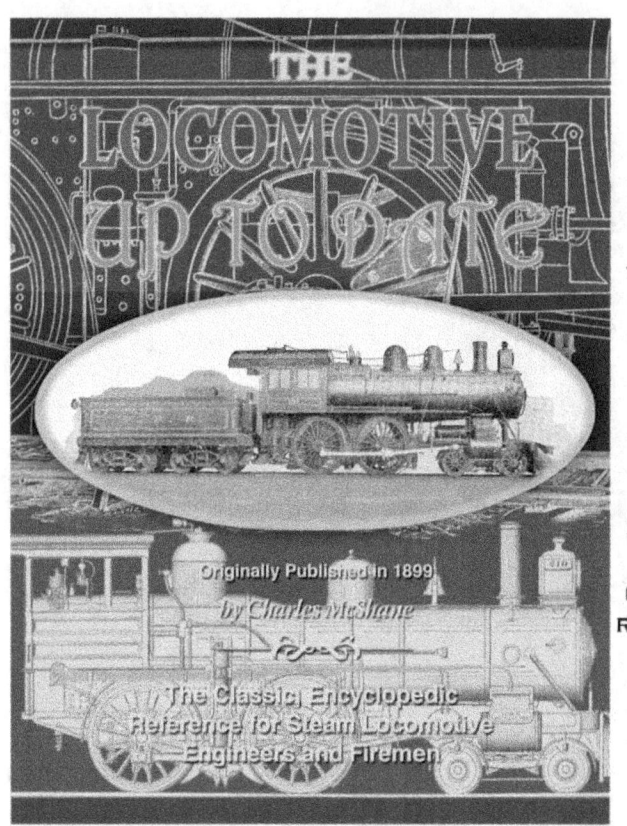

When it was originally published in 1899, **The Locomotive Up to Date** was hailed as "...the most definitive work ever published concerning the mechanism that has transformed the American nation: the steam locomotive." Filled with over 700 pages of text, diagrams and photos, this remains one of the most important railroading books ever written. From steam valves to sanders, trucks to side rods, it's a treasure trove of information, explaining in easy-to-understand language how the most sophisticated machines of the 19th Century were operated and maintained. This new edition is an exact duplicate of the original. Reformatted as an easy-to-read 8.5x11 volume, it's delightful for railroad enthusiasts of all ages.

Originally printed in 1898 and then periodically revised, **The Motorman...and His Duties** served as the definitive training text for a generation of streetcar operators. A must-have for the trolley or train enthusiast, it is also an important source of information for museum staff and docents. Lavishly illustrated with numerous photos and black and white line drawings, this affordable reprint contains all of the original text. Includes chapters on trolley car types and equipment, troubleshooting, brakes, controllers, electricity and principles, electric traction, multi-car control and has a convenient glossary in the back. If you've ever operated a trolley car, or just had an electric train set, this is a terrific book for your shelf!

ALSO NOW AVAILABLE FROM PERISCOPEFILM.COM!

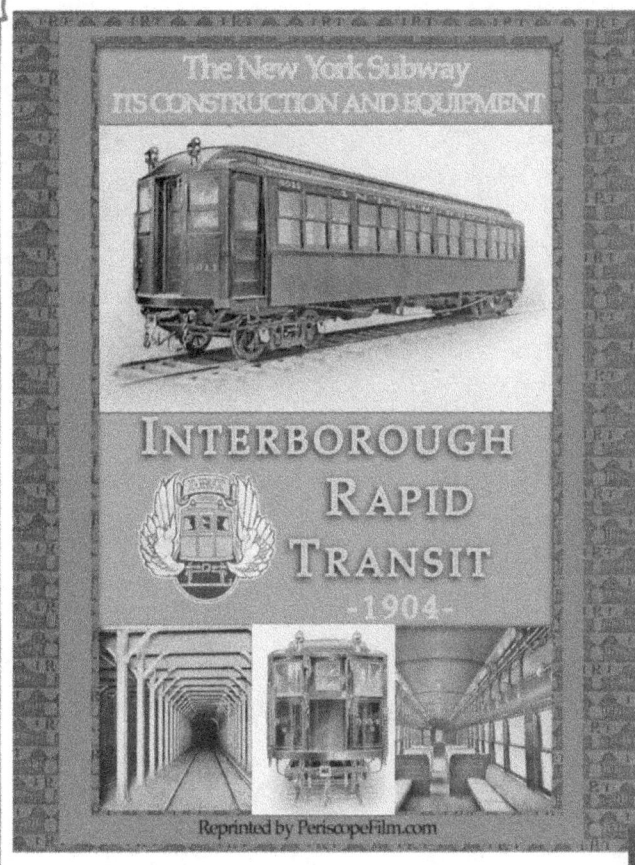

On October 27, 1904, the Interborough Rapid Transit Company opened the first subway in New York City. Running between City Hall and 145th Street at Broadway, the line was greeted with enthusiasm and, in some circles, trepidation. Created under the supervision of Chief Engineer S.L.F. Deyo, the arrival of the IRT foreshadowed the end of the "elevated" transit era on the island of Manhattan. The subway proved such a success that the IRT Co. soon achieved a monopoly on New York public transit. In 1940 the IRT and its rival the BMT were taken over by the City of New York. Today, the IRT subway lines still exist, primarily in Manhattan where they are operated as the "A Division" of the subway. Reprinted here is a special book created by the IRT, recounting the design and construction of the fledgling subway system. Originally created in 1904, it presents the IRT story with a flourish, and with numerous fascinating illustrations and rare photographs.

Originally written in the late 1900's and then periodically revised, A History of the Baldwin Locomotive Works chronicles the origins and growth of one of America's greatest industrial-era corporations. Founded in the early 1830's by Philadelphia jeweler Matthais Baldwin, the company built a huge number of steam locomotives before ceasing production in 1949. These included the 4-4-0 American type, 2-8-2 Mikado and 2-8-0 Consolidation. Hit hard by the loss of the steam engine market, Baldwin soldiered on for a brief while, producing electric and diesel engines. General Electric's dominance of the market proved too much, and Baldwin finally closed its doors in 1956. By that time over 70,500 Baldwin locomotives had been produced. This high quality reprint of the official company history dates from 1920. The book has been slightly reformatted, but care has been taken to preserve the integrity of the text.

NOW AVAILABLE AT
WWW.PERISCOPEFILM.COM

©2007-2010 Periscope Film LLC
All Rights Reserved
ISBN 978-1-935700-12-8
www.PeriscopeFilm.com

www.ingramcontent.com/pod-product-compliance
Lightning Source LLC
LaVergne TN
LVHW061347060426
835512LV00012B/2595